Congratulations on the arrival of your beautiful baby!

ENDLESS LOVE

Printed in the United Kingdom.
First Edition: July, 2024
ISBN: 9798328210218

Head to head and nose to nose
I love holding you so close

Cheek to cheek and mouth to ear
Whispering, "I love you, dear"

Through the stormy, cloudy night
I am always by your side

Endless love will be our guide
Through the dark till morning light

Gentle breathing oh so sweet
Tiny hands gripping the sheet

Little murmurs in your sleep
In my palm, your strong heartbeat

Nothing in this world compares
To the love a mother shares

Love so pure, unbreakable
Fills us and is growing still

Nothing in this world compares
To the way a mother cares

Giving body, mind and soul
This true love making her whole

Heartbeats sound the melody
of love lasting eternally

And with every caring kiss
Softly whispered promises

For each laugh and every tear
In your journey, I'll be near

Teach you kindness, patience, grace
to be curious and brave

Make you confident and strong
Help you through and carry on

Be your anchor and your cheer
Whisper courage in your ear

Innocence and purest light
Shining from your eyes so bright

You're a wonder in my arm
Pure and precious, gentle charm

Nothing ever felt so true
As the love I feel for you

In your presence, I am shown
How to guide my soul back home.

A note from the Author:

May your home forever be blessed with

Endless Love

THE TIMELESS BONDS SERIES

by Katia Peel

Timeless Bonds: Celebrating Life and Love is a heartwarming series that rejoices in the arrival of new babies. This beautifully crafted collection includes three enchanting books, each dedicated to celebrating the unique bonds formed between new parents and their babies:

Endless Love: The gentle ode to the profound connection between new mums and their babies. This book captures the tender moments that define motherhood, with loving words and exquisite pencil drawings that make it a perfect gift for new mums.

Boundless Love: A heartfelt tribute to the special bond between new dads and their newborns. This book is an ideal gift for new dads, filled with poetry that touches the heart and soul and illustrations of doting fathers with their babies.

Everlasting Love: A celebration of new families and the joy of welcoming a baby into the world. This book features poems that nurture the family bond and beautiful illustrations of parents and their babies, making it a cherished keepsake for new families.

Each book in the ***Timeless Bonds*** series is perfect for commemorating the miracle of life and love.

Printed in Great Britain
by Amazon

52520733R00016